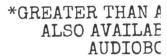

CW00821053

*GREATER THAN A
ALSO AVAILAE
AUDIOBC

Greater Than a Tourist
Book Series
Reviews from Readers

I think the series is wonderful and beneficial for tourists to get information before visiting the city.

-Seckin Zumbul, Izmir Turkey

I am a world traveler who has read many trip guides but this one really made a difference for me. I would call it a heartfelt creation of a local guide expert instead of just a guide.

-Susy, Isla Holbox, Mexico

New to the area like me, this is a must have!

-Joe, Bloomington, USA

This is a good series that gets down to it when looking for things to do at your destination without having to read a novel for just a few ideas.

-Rachel, Monterey, USA

Good information to have to plan my trip to this destination.

-Pennie Farrell, Mexico

Great ideas for a port day.

-Mary Martin USA

Aptly titled, you won't just be a tourist after reading this book. You'll be greater than a tourist!

-Alan Warner, Grand Rapids, USA

Even though I only have three days to spend in San Miguel in an upcoming visit, I will use the author's suggestions to guide some of my time there. An easy read - with chapters named to guide me in directions I want to go.

-Robert Catapano, USA

Great insights from a local perspective! Useful information and a very good value!

-Sarah, USA

This series provides an in-depth experience through the eyes of a local. Reading these series will help you to travel the city in with confidence and it'll make your journey a unique one.

-Andrew Teoh, Ipoh, Malaysia

GREATER THAN A TOURIST- LONDON ONTARIO CANADA

50 Travel Tips from a Local

Yoda Olinyk

The statements in this book are of the authors and may not be the views of CZYK Publishing or Greater Than a Tourist.

First Edition

Cover designed by: Ivana Stamenkovic

Cover Image:
https://en.wikipedia.org/wiki/File:London_Ontario_Skyline_Panorama.jpg

Image 1: https://en.wikipedia.org/wiki/File:LONDONMORNING.jpg
Image 2: https://en.wikipedia.org/wiki/File:London_Life_Headquarters.jpg
Image 3: https://en.wikipedia.org/wiki/File:Thames_River_Springbank_Park.jpg
Image 4:
https://en.wikipedia.org/wiki/File:Wellington_Road_Downtown_London.jpg

CZYK Publishing Since 2011.
CZYKPublishing.com
Greater Than a Tourist

Mill Hall, PA
All rights reserved.
ISBN: 9798351928623

>TOURIST

50 TRAVEL TIPS FROM A LOCAL

BOOK DESCRIPTION

With travel tips and culture in our guidebooks written by a local, it is never too late to visit London. Greater Than a Tourist-London Ontario Canada by Yoda Olinyk offers the inside scoop on "The Other London" Most travel books tell you how to travel like a tourist. Although there is nothing wrong with that, as part of the 'Greater Than a Tourist' series, this book will give you candid travel tips from someone who has lived at your next travel destination. This guide book will not tell you exact addresses or store hours but instead gives you knowledge that you may not find in other smaller print travel books. Experience cultural, culinary delights, and attractions with the guidance of a Local. Slow down and get to know the people with this invaluable guide. By the time you finish this book, you will be eager and prepared to discover new activities at your next travel destination.

Inside this travel guide book you will find:
 Visitor information from a Local

 Tour ideas and inspiration

 Valuable guidebook information

Greater Than a Tourist- A Travel Guidebook with 50 Travel Tips from a Local. Slow down, stay in one place, and get to know the people and culture. By the time you finish this book, you will be eager and prepared to travel to your next destination.

OUR STORY

Traveling is a passion of the Greater than a Tourist book series creator. Lisa studied abroad in college, and for their honeymoon Lisa and her husband toured Europe. During her travels to Malta, an older man tried to give her some advice based on his own experience living on the island since he was a young boy. She was not sure if she should talk to the stranger but was interested in his advice. When traveling to some places she was wary to talk to locals because she was afraid that they weren't being genuine. Through her travels, Lisa learned how much locals had to share with tourists. Lisa created the Greater Than a Tourist book series to help connect people with locals. A topic that locals are very passionate about sharing.

TABLE OF CONTENTS

DEDICATION

This books is dedicated to
all those who love to get lost.

ABOUT THE AUTHOR

Yoda Olinyk is a chef and writer who lives in London, Ontario. Born and raised in the small town of Thorndale, not far from London, Yoda remembers the weekend trips her family would take into "the big city" for shopping and groceries. From visits to Apple Land and Masonville mall, to go carting at East Park or bowling at Bowlerama— there was always something fun to do in the city.

Yoda left her small town roots at the age of 18 to attend culinary school a few hours away, and then began traveling and working abroad, but she always knew she would return to her roots. Her work brought her back to the city of London where she owns and operates the city's only plant-based catering company, Yoda's Kitchen. She also works as a freelance writer and in 2020, she published her first book *Salt and Sour*. This book is a blend of her two loves... food and words!

HOW TO USE THIS BOOK

The *Greater Than a Tourist* book series was written by someone who has lived in an area for over three months. The goal of this book is to help travelers either dream or experience different locations by providing opinions from a local. The author has made suggestions based on their own experiences. Please check before traveling to the area in case the suggested places are unavailable.

Travel Advisories: As a first step in planning any trip abroad, check the Travel Advisories for your intended destination.
https://travel.state.gov/content/travel/en/
traveladvisories/traveladvisories.html

FROM THE PUBLISHER

Traveling can be one of the most important parts of a person's life. The anticipation and memories that you have are some of the best. As a publisher of the Greater Than a Tourist, as well as the popular *50 Things to Know* book series, we strive to help you learn about new places, spark your imagination, and inspire you. Wherever you are and whatever you do I wish you safe, fun, and inspiring travel.

Lisa Rusczyk Ed. D.
CZYK Publishing

WELCOME TO
> TOURIST

London Life's Headquarters in Downtown London

A look at downtown London during a winter morning.

The Thames River in Springbank Park — London, Ontario

Wellington Street in Downtown London

"Not all who wander are lost..."

When most people hear the word "London," they think about Buckingham Palace, The Tower of London, staunch traditions, art and a bustling subway system a.k.a. the "tube." When I tell people I am from London, I can always see their eyes light up until I correct them and say, "Oh, no, the other London."

The London in Ontario, Canada is known by many as "The Other London" but for locals, we just call it The Forest City. London, Ontario is a lush, culturally diverse, gorgeous city located right in the middle of Toronto and Detroit. London is unique in the sense that it is located so close to two huge metropolises but has a true "small town" feel. With 6 different, uniquely special neighborhoods and just a short drive to three of the great lakes, there is always something to do in the Forest City!

When you wander the streets of London, you will see faces from all over the world. London has a rich cultural history and is home to dozens of great ethnic restaurants. London also has a thriving music scene, and is the center of festival season come summer.

No matter what your reason for coming to London — whether it's a concert at the famous Bud Gardens, a festival at Victoria Park, a sporting event or an exhibit at the museum, London, Ontario has a lot to offer! It may not be London, England, but we do have a Thames River running through our beautiful city, and some of our own traditions which you will discover throughout this book.

So get on your walking shoes and be prepared to wander the Forest City with us… and remember, not all who wander are lost… but if you want to get lost in the Forest City, you'll have a great time while doing it!

London
Ontario, Canada

London
Ontario
Canada
Climate

	High	Low
January	27	14
February	29	14
March	39	24
April	53	35
May	66	45
June	75	54
July	80	59
August	78	57
September	70	50
October	57	40
November	45	32
December	33	21

GreaterThanaTourist.com

Temperatures are in Fahrenheit degrees.
Source: NOAA

1. TAKE A WALK IN VICTORIA PARK

Stroll through the idyllic park that is right in the center of London's downtown core. This park connected the four busiest corners of downtown London, and is at the heart of the financial district and the home of several festivals from May-October. In December, the park is transformed into a winter wonderland so there is always something to do while in Victoria Park. Join the walkers or joggers and get some exercise, or be like me and grab a seat to people watch from one of the best seats in the city! Make sure to stop by the tank at the northwest corner of the park and check out many of the historic plaques, benches and statues along the way. Victoria Park has a rich history and is so much more than just a beautiful gathering place — it is where the British Garrison Troops were stationed during the 1837 Upper Canada Rebellion and in World War 1 and 2, respectively.

2. SHOP AND EAT AT THE WESTERN FAIR FARMER'S MARKET

There are many Saturday markets worth checking out in London, Ontario, but the Western Fair Market is the one that can't be missed! This market is a cornerstone of London's local food economy and is also a great place to bring the whole family! This market offers lots of free parking and is open every Saturday and Sunday for the whole year. In summer, it is overflowing with local vegetables, cheeses and meats, and year round you can find local gifts, artisan breads and more. One of my favourite things to do is stop by Momos for some Nepalese tea and momos, and then if there's room in my belly, grab a few pupusas from True Taco which is a legendary El Salvadorian restaurant in London. I also love to pick up some biscuits for my dog which are homemade and affordable. I rarely leave the market without some fresh flowers, too!

Make sure to leave lots of time and head upstairs while you're at the market... there is a whole separate market on the upper floor of this building teeming with everything from clothing to crystals to books and more.

3. WITNESS THE "FLAME OF HOPE"

The flame of hope sits on Adelaide Street, near Queen Street, in downtown London and is a symbol of hope for anyone who suffers from diabetes. It was erected 1989 to honour Sir Frederick Banting's discovery of insulin and will burn until a cure is found for diabetes. It was lit in the presence of Queen Elizabeth and is a site to see if you're downtown London.

4. GORGE ON RIBS AT LONDON'S RIB FEST

London, Ontario is home of the second biggest Rib Festival in North America (and the biggest in Canada)! If you're wondering what a rib festival is… it is just what is sounds like… rib lovers from all over the world flock to this festival to cook and eat ribs!

During July when the festival takes place (Victoria Park), the entire downtown core smells like barbeque sauce and smoke! If you attend this festival, make sure you check out the other food options and grab a seat at a picnic table for one of the peaceful summer nights London is famous for!

5. DRIVE TO ONE OF THE MANY NEARBY BEACHES

London is the perfect location for families and beach lovers because it is a short 40-50 minute drive away from several iconic beaches. Situated right in between Lake Huron and Lake Erie, you can easily access many of Ontario's most beautiful beaches — Port Stanley, Port Bruce, Grand Bend and Ipperwash, just to name a few! There are also smaller beaches and provincial parks less than an hour from London which are worth checking out and where I spent a lot of my childhood. Port Franks was always a favourite, as well as Long Point.

If you're in London for the summer and you're a beach lover, make sure you take advantage of these super close beaches... and might we recommend stopping at Shaw's Ice-cream on the way?

6. LAUGH ALONG TO SOME LIVE COMEDY

I love catching a show at Centennial Hall which has hosted famous comedians such as Jerry Seinfeld, Bo Burnham, Bill Burr and many others over the years. If you're interested in the art of live comedy, you can also find smaller comedy shows and open mics around the city where locals will try their luck at making you laugh. This is one my favourite things to do on a weekend in the city.

London is also home of Yuk Yuk's comedy so no matter where you stay in London, there are some laughs to be had nearby!

7. BEER LOVERS REJOICE! LONDON HAS YOU COVERED!

A few years ago, Londoners decided they really loved to make amazing beer! In the last decade, several craft breweries have been established here and they are not to be missed on your tour of the Forest City. In Old East Village alone, there are three incredible breweries just five minutes for each other, so if you're looking to do a day of exploring some of the best beers London has to offer, make sure to stop by Powerhouse Brewing, Anderson Ales and the London Brew Co-op. They all have fantastic patios and on weekends, you can often find live music and events here.

London is also home to the Labatt brewery and packaging facility and ships famous beers such as Labatt Blue, Alexander Keiths and Budweiser. This world renowned brewery offers tours and tastings, so it is worthwhile to make it a stop on your brewery tour of London.

8. TAKE THE KIDS TO STORYBOOK GARDENS

If you grew up in London, you probably have a story about Storybook Gardens. It is an iconic family-friendly theme park and nursery located in the hamlet of Byron, close to Springbank Park. This place has it all—a petting zoo, rides, play pens, water park and more! This park is also unique because of its quiet and tranquil location (Springbank Park), there is something here for kids and grown-ups alike and should not be missed while in London.

9. SEE A SHOW AT LONDON FRINGE

London is known for supporting its artists, and Fringe Festival is no exception. Fringe is a worldwide festival for artists of all kinds to showcase their work in a safe, dynamic and celebratory environment, so when Fringe comes to London, Londoners get on board! It's got everything from live plays, music, dance and magic shows, so if you're in town for this festival you are bound to have a great time. If you're

a night owl, make sure to check out Nuit Blanche —
the festival that lasts all night!

10. COMICON AND COMIC BOOK STORES

It's hard to know exactly why Londoners love comics so much, but London, Ontario is home to half a dozen comic book stores. L.A Mood, Heroes and World's Away just to name a few... but London also hosts its own version of ComiCon every year where you can find collectibles and cos play. If you're in London on May 6th and consider yourself a comic book fan, then make sure you're up early to get in line at any one of these shops for Free Comic Book Day (observed nationwide, but is particularly special in London, where people line up down several city blocks for their free comic!)

11. BUDWEISER GARDENS — MORE THAN JUST AN EPIC CONCERT VENUE

Budweiser Gardens or, as the locals call it, Bud Gardens, has had many different names and hosted thousands of huge concerts and events including Bob Dylan, The Foo Fighters, U2 and more. It is also the home of the London Knights and London Lightening, our hockey and basketball teams, respectively. If you're in London, make sure you stop by to see the site where Johnny Cash famously proposed to June Carter on stage (at the time called London Gardens.) If you're in town to go to Bud Gardens, make sure you leave extra time to find parking — it is located in the downtown core and free parking fills up very quickly! Also leave time to eat at one of the many iconic restaurants nearby including JD's, The Works, Zenza Pizza and more!

12. VISIT THE HISTORICAL (AND BEAUTIFUL!) ELDON HOUSE

Known to Londoners as Eldon, Eldon House is the oldest continued residence in London, Ontario. It was built in 1834 and given to the city in 1959. It was named after the Earl of Eldon by its original owners and the city kept its name. It is situated in London's prettiest park, Harris Park, and is the home of Canada Day and Victoria Day fireworks, as well as other culturally significant celebrations. You can take a tour of the grounds, or just grab a seat in the picturesque Harris Park and admire the building from afar, while dreaming of what life might have been like in 1834.

13. CATCH A LONDON MAJOR'S GAME AT LABATT PARK

What can we say? London, Ontario is passionate about sports! And The London Majors are our team! This independent, minor league team is famous around London and was inducted into the Sports Hall of Fame in 2015. In 2006, they were named the first all-star team and in 2019, their general manager Roop Chanderdat reached over 300 wins in his tenure. You can experience your own London Major's magic at a home game which are played at the historic Labatt Park, which is the oldest operating baseball stadium... in the world!! If you're a baseball lover and want to witness a pro-game in an approachable, small-town setting, this is an experience that should not be missed.

14. FOR YOUR FOUR-LEGGED FRIENDS, DON'T MISS PAWLOOZA!

Every year, London hosts a very special event for man's best friend... Pawlooza is the ultimate festival for dogs and dog lovers. The date changes every year, so check for updates, but this event draws in 25,000 people each year (and 6000 dogs!) At the festival, you can expect to find everything you need to know about training, adoption, healthy food options are more. There are also plenty of activities for your furry friends, including agility courses, swimming and play pens. My 10-year-old mixed lab can vouch for Pawlooza as a "must" for your dog if the timing works out. This is a great event that is pay-by-donation, which raises money for a variety of organizations in London that need funding to help dogs live happy and healthy lives. If you're in London and you love animals, this is the festival for you!

15. STROLL THROUGH WORTLEY VILLAGE

Voted one of the top places to live in Canada, Wortley village takes its reputation very seriously! Sometimes called, Old South, Wortley village attracts people of all ages and backgrounds with its small town feel, right in the heart of our big city. Wortley Village is just a few streets wide and walkable in 20 minutes or less, but when you're in the core, you'll definitely see what all the fuss is about. Stop at one of the art galleries or shops, dine at some of the city's coolest restaurants (sushi, vegan, you name it, Wortley has it!) or get coffee at the quaint outdoor patio at The Black Walnut café. If you're traveling with your dog, bring them along! It seems like everyone in Wortley Village either has a dog or loves dogs — many of the shops and cafes are dog friendly.

16. LET FANSHAWE COLLEGE'S CHEF STUDENTS COOK YOU DINNER

Located just off their downtown campus, The Chef's Table is a unique dining experience worth mentioning. Fanshawe College has a unique training model where their students will spend some of their curriculum getting hands on culinary experience by working at this restaurant. It is a great opportunity to not only support London's student culture, but you'll also get a great meal out of it. Speaking as a Fanshawe College Alumni (along with 11% of London's population over the age of 25,) I can definitely recommend this restaurant as a great dining option that is often missed.

17. EXPLORE LONDON'S RICH LITERARY SCENE

Although London is the birthplace of many famous writers (Emma Donoghue, Orlo Miller and Vanessa Brown, just to name a few!) we don't tend to brag about it too much. Instead, London is the home of some fantastic literary events and bookstores. If you're a writer, check out WordFest which is free and takes place every November. If you're an avid reader, then you must stop by Brown and Dickson, Attic Books and the famous City Lights Bookshop. All of these locally owned stores have that "old bookstore" feel with shelves lined with every book you could ever dream of. If you're a book lover, it would be easy to spend days exploring the city's bookshops, and make sure you check out one of the many cafés where you can curl up and read with an exceptional cup of joe!

18. LONDONERS ARE FULL OF GAY PRIDE!

London Pride is a huge deal around here. Typically taking place in June or July, London Pride is a festival that supports and celebrates gay culture and the entire SLGBTQIA+ community. There is an entire week of events which include dance parties, poetry nights, community engagement and concerts, but the real party is always on the day of the Pride Parade. People and businesses from far and wide come dressed in their brightest clothes, to show their support of the SLGBTQIA+ community here in London. The parade moves through the downtown core and encourages cars to honk and people to cheer to show their support. All of Pride London encourages safety and inclusion, so if you're in London when it's on, make sure to attend!

19. DINE AT ONE OF THE MANY GREAT RESTAURANTS ON RICHMOND ROW

If you asked any Londoner where they love to eat, you might get a variety of replies... but if you ask them where there are the most restaurants to choose from, they will tell you: Richmond Row! Walkable in a few blocks (and part of Victoria Park), Richmond Row is the perfect place to go to see what London, Ontario's chefs have to offer. Stop at Barney's famous outdoor patio for a cold one; get real fish and chips at one of the many Irish Pubs; try Indian or Thai if spice is your thing. If you're craving a Burger, there are a few places to choose from, plus pizza, vegan food and street food.

If you're looking for something a little more high-end and a great glass of wine, make sure to check out Garlics of London, The Tasting Room or The Church Key... all of these restaurants have been around for a long time and have great reputations. If you choose Garlics, do not leave without trying their garlic ice-cream, or enjoy dessert on the walk back at one of the frozen yogurt shops and take in more of the city.

Note that parking can be very difficult downtown London, but especially on Richmond Row. In all of London, there are less than 850 paid parking spaces per 100,000 residents, so parking spots are highly coveted! It may be best to take a taxi to avoid driving around if you're not familiar with the area.

20. YOU'LL LOVE THE INTERNATIONAL FOOD FESTIVAL

Every weekend in the summer, Victoria park is filled with a new festival — from Sunfest to Rib Fest... but The International Food Festival is one that Londoners love the most, and we think you will too... especially if you like to try new and exciting foods! At this festival, trucks and street food vendors line the park with everything from Polish pierogi, to Thai noodles, to Eritrean Ful... there is truly something for everyone at this lively event! There is also live music, beautiful, authentic clothing and plenty of family and pet friendly events throughout the weekend. I make a point to go every single year and always find something new to eat.

21. TAKE IN A SHOW AT THE GRAND THEATER

The Grand Theater is an age-old tradition for many Londoners. With shows year round, this theater has the heart of many locals. Take in a show like Alice in Wonderland, The Little Mermaid or The Wizard of Oz and watch local performers on their home stage. Make sure to purchase your tickets ahead of time, especially in December, and give yourself time for dinner AND a show. Many of the nearby restaurants provide deals for ticket-holders and so it's easy to make a whole night of it. My favourite show so far was The Wizard of Oz, but I continue to add to my list at this iconic London venue.

22. GIVE BACK AT 'GROWING CHEF'S ONTARIO'

Growing Chefs Ontario is a not-for-profit business located in the heart of downtown London. Its philosophy is all about teaching young kids about the importance of real food and food sovereignty... but their work goes well beyond that! This organization launched by going into children's classrooms (as young as Grade 1) and doing quick cooking demos, all while making vegetables fun for even the pickiest eaters. They have since expanded and operate a full service restaurant and catering company (The Beet Café) and employ dozens of youth in the community. This organization is still largely volunteer run, so many local chefs volunteer for their summer pizza nights, or cooking classes. Check out their events calendar and you may just find yourself being cooked for by one of the city's famous chefs!

The best part is all of the money raised goes right back into the community so by choosing Growing Chefs as one of your stops, you really are giving back.

23. TAKE THE KIDDOS TO THE CHILDREN'S MUSEUM

The Children's Museum is famous with London's littles! An epic play place but also a place to learn and grow! If you're interested in taking your kids here, make sure you check online for their schedule and sign up early, especially during the summer months when camps book up quickly. Your kids will love the famous Whale Tale and crafts room.

24. LEARN OUR HISTORY AT THE WOLSELEY BARRACKS

Book a tour of the Royal Canadian Regiment Museum located at The Wolseley Barracks in London, Ontario and be prepared for more than just a history lesson! This interactive museum provides education through its prized collection of documents, pictures, books and artifacts (including several tanks). This tour is family friendly and educational, so make sure you call ahead to book.

25. SUPPORT THE AEOLIAN HALL HERITAGE BUILDING

Known to locals simply as, The Aeolian or Aeolian Hall, this place holds a lot of nostalgia for many Londoners. Built in 1884, and located in the heart of Old East Village at 795 Dundas Street, The Aeolian is as historic as they come. Originally meant to be offices, this venue was turned into a local concert venue suitable only for small, intimate shows. Some huge artists have come from all over the world to play shows for 100 people in this super intimate venue because the acoustics are said to be some of the very best! If you ever have the chance to attend a show here, it is a must-do while in London. Every ticket sale goes into preserving the building and supporting the upkeep of this very old venue. It is also volunteer led, some ticket prices are always reasonable and donations can be made anytime. Some of my very favourite concerts have taken place at The Aeolian so I make sure to donate every time I go.

26. TAKE A HIKE AT FANSHAWE LAKE

Fanshawe Lake is situated just east of the city of London, but feels like it is hours away. This hike is tranquil and quiet, and is open year round. Although only certain sections of the trail are maintained in the winter, it is a great place for snowshoeing or cross country skiing. In warmer months, you can hike or bike the entire 22km trail (beginner level, mostly flat terrain) or just take in a small section. You can also check out the Fanshawe Dam. Either way, this is not to be missed for nature lovers visiting London. There are many local birds to take in, and during the spring you might even find some wild mushrooms!

27. PLACE YOUR BETS AT GATEWAY CASINO

Although the casino in London is small, it has everything a gambler wants… slots, tables and racing. Drop in anytime or make a whole night of it and attend a Yuk Yuk's show, go for dinner at their restaurant, take in a show and then place your bets!

28. THE ANNUAL WESTERN FAIR SHOULD NOT BE MISSED!

Every September, London hosts the Western Fair at the Western Fair Grounds, near Old East Village. Some families go every single year because it is a great place to make family memories, but also because there is something new every year! From their annual pig race, to the derby, to the petting zoo and of course the rides, there is something from everyone at this fair. One of my favourite traditions about going to the fair is getting Di's Fry Cart Fries and eating them while on the ferris wheel overlooking the city's core, If you're more adventurous than me, you could ride the Gravatron or go for a tour of the fun house. This fair is family friendly and is a place you can just drop in, or you can by weekend passes for all the events online ahead of time. There are also concerts in the band shell and a talent show every year.

29. GOAT YOGA, RETREATS AND MORE

London is situated between many rural towns so there are many farming communities nearby. At one of those farms, you can partake in something called Goat Yoga, which is exactly as fun as it sounds! London also has a rich spiritual community so there are plenty of places offering regular yoga, hot yoga, meditation retreats and more. Check out The Covent Garden Market on Wednesday mornings for free outdoor yoga, or the crystal room at Purdy Natural.

30. GO KNIGHTS GO!

There is nothing that will show you how much Londoners love their city more than going to a Knights game! The London Knights play their home games at Budweiser Gardens but also play provincially during their winter season and make every Londoner proud every single time they win a game. In December, bring a kid's toy with you to the game and take part in the Teddy Toss, where Londoners come together to collect toys for those

who need a little help during the holiday season.
While at a game, enjoy a hot dog and wear green and
gold if you want to feel like a true local… and make
sure you know the chant… GO Knights GO!

31. VEGAN FOOD ABOUND IN LONDON, ONTARIO!

Londoners are a healthy bunch… so many
Londoners love eating healthy food. That's where the
city's vegan scene really gets to shine. London has
plenty of plant-based restaurants to choose from so if
you're in town and that's your thing, you will have
plenty of variety. In Wortley Village, check out Plant
Matter Kitchen for pub fare and healthy entrees. If
you're feeling something super hearty, check out The
V Food Spot, and Copper Branch if you're looking
for salad. There are also plenty of vegan meet-ups and
groups located in London Ontario such as Plant
Empowered London and Veg Fest so if you're in
London and need a plant-based suggestion, there are
lots of places to go for recommendations.

32. VISIT THE LANDMARK PALACE THEATER

The Palace Theater may not look fancy on the outside, but it has a whole lot of heart! This theater is fully accessible and offers a wide range of live performances (book ahead of time) as well as film screenings of movies you may not have seen in a while. The Palace is a huge supporter of local art and music, and hosts The Fringe Festival events each year. It also happens to such an old facility, when it opened, it only showed silent films... no joke!

33. GET READY FOR A BLAST FROM THE PAST AT FANSHAWE PIONEER VILLAGE

This history museum is unlike any other. You will enter through Fanshawe Conservation Area and as soon as you pull in, you will understand their slogan, "Where the past is the present." This museum aims to recreate Canadian lifestyles from 1820-1920. You will be greeted by Pioneer People wearing traditional clothes and bonnets, and will be taken on a tour of the

Heritage Village which includes 19th century homes and traditions. At this historical venue, there are a variety of demonstrations to see including churning butter, tapping maple trees, wood chopping, candle making and more. This is a family friendly day trip that should be booked ahead of time.

34. SPRINGBANK PARK AND CEMETERY

The largest park and trail in London, Springbank Park stretches from one end of the city to the other. On the well-manicured trail you will find dog parks, scenic vistas, river crossings and you will also pass through the Springbank Cemetery which is the oldest in the city. This trail is safe for bikers, joggers and pets. You can enter at many locations and it is well-lit, busy and safe for people of all ages. I like to go for bird-watching, people watching, a workout, a view of the river and more.

35. THE BOHO NIGHT MARKET BAZAAR

Hosted by two local business owners, this summer festival is not to be missed! Dates vary year to year, but these night markets typically happen once a month, on Thursday evenings, throughout the summer. They are hosted at 111 Mount Pleasant Ave and from the moment you walk into the yard, you will be transported to another place. Inspired by Indian Bazaars, this market is full of local artisans and producers, with a focus on small businesses and women-run businesses, especially. You will not only find eclectic music and amazing food vendors, but you can also purchase everything from crystals and mandalas, to all natural soaps, perfumes and potions, to books and records... this market has it all! It is typically free and pop-up style so if you're interested in going, keep your eyes open for their next date.

36. VISIT THE COVENT GARDEN MARKET

This downtown market was of course named and modeled after the famous Covent Garden in London, England, but we think you'll find this market just as exciting. I could easily spend an hour at the cheese counter alone. With vendors selling everything from fresh fruits and vegetables, to sushi and smoothies and everything in between, you can easily grab a quick lunch to enjoy picnic style or dine in at one of the many restaurants. Also check out upstairs for tea, more shopping and The Original Kid's Company for a show! Note that the Covent Garden Market is one of the only places downtown with free parking.

37. THE BIGGEST FESTIVAL EVER... SUN FEST!

Okay, Sun Fest is technically the second biggest festival in Ontario, but it is definitely the biggest festival for Londoners! Catch one of the concerts in the outdoor band shell, walk through the park people watching, eat a plethora of street food and shop for international treasures. Vendors come from across the world to share their fares and trinkets and this festival has a real vibe that you have to see it to feel it. Sun Fest is free, family friendly and takes place every July in Victoria Park.

38. BOLER MOUNTAIN... SO MUCH MORE THAN JUST SKIING!

Boler Mountain is a well-known ski resort for Londoners and ski lovers all around, but did you also know that Boler Mountain is open year round and has TONS of activities for the whole family?! Try your hands at zip-lining or take to the trails for a scenic hike. Boler Mountain does require tickets to be purchased, so make sure you budget for this. While you're there, check out the quaint little hamlet of Byron where the ski hill is located in and try one of their coffee shops or walking trails.

39. THE CLASSIC DRIVE-IN... A MUST!

Head to The Mustang Drive-In to take in not one, but two movies—open every weekend. If it's been a while since you went to the drive-in, this will be a special treat. Purchase your tickets ahead of time or try your luck and roll up... set your stations, get your popcorn and enjoy a classic movie experience! You can find all the movie show times and listings online.

40. DON'T LET THE NAME FOOL YOU, THE SIFTON BOG IS A MAGICAL PLACE!

Located in west London, The Sifton Bog is more than just a bog. With luscious hiking trails, steep hills and yes, a bog, this is a nature walk that has it all. The bog was created by glacial patterns which allowed for aquatic life to thrive during the Ice Age, so it is a pretty magical place. It's also dog and kid friendly; some of this trail is considered intermediate for hikers, with some steep hills and waterways to cross, but there is also a flat area with benches for book reading or bird watching.

Some other great hiking spots in London include: Warbler Woods, the Meadowlilly Trail, Westminister Ponds, The Coves, Sharon's Creek and Kilally Meadows.

41. ADDIS ABABAS: GO FOR THE FOOD, LEAVE WITH AN UNFORGETTABLE EXPERIENCE

Without fail, this restaurant is this author's all-time favourite in the city. It's a bit of a hidden gem — located just outside of downtown and not a lot of people know about it... but if you're looking for a truly amazing experience during your stay in London, then dinner at Addis Ababas is key. This Ethiopian restaurant serves the best, most authentic African cuisine. From lovely owners and the best coffee (roasted right at your table!) your entire meal will be an experience you won't forget. You will be served injera bread and instructed to eat with your hands. With so many flavours and textures to choose from, you will be guaranteed to leave happy and full... and you WILL want to come back.

42. LONDON IS A CANADIAN CITY, EH? BUT SOME THINGS MIGHT BE DIFFERENT AROUND HERE...

Although many Canadians are bilingual, you will find most Londoners speak English as their first language. London is home to many different cultures, backgrounds and languages, so when you're walking the streets or exploring, you will hear a plethora of languages and accents. When in doubt, English is a safe bet.

London businesses do business in Canadian dollars. We use the Loonie ($1) and Toonie ($2) coin which might be new to you if you're traveling from far away or used to American currency. Basically it's the same, but a lot heavier in your pocket!

Most of Ontario, including London is in the Eastern Standard Time zone and adheres to British English writing and typing practices (meaning you might see things spelt in a peculiar way at times.)

43. GETTING AROUND...
SAFETY, FIRST!

London, Ontario is considered to be a fairly safe city, but as with any travel, you should ensure you always know your route and what to do in case of an emergency. London has three large hospitals and operates its emergency system using 9-1-1 as the fire and medical emergency phone number. As with any city, there are certain areas you may want to avoid walking alone at night, so it is also good to download Uber if adventuring at night. London does not have subway system, but does have an extensive bus system with over 190 buses and 42 routes, and a lot of them run until midnight 7 days a week. London also has an International Airport (small, but mighty!) and a VIA Rail train station.

44. DON'T MISS THE LONDON AIR SHOW!

Watch the famous Thunderbird jets take a sky dive and zip around the London skyline in this annual air show that draws thousands of airplane enthusiasts and thrill seekers from around the country. You can head to the event and purchase tickets or if you're really lucky (like I was when I was a child!) to live near the airport, you can set up some lawn chairs and catch a free show from the back patio! Either way, this September event is one you won't want to skip out on if you're in London.

45. PUMPKIN-SPICE LOVERS GATHER AT APPLE LAND

I have fond memories of running through the rows of apples during the fall months with my siblings, but have enjoyed my time at Apple Land just as much as an adult. There is a corn maze, apple picking (ladders and buckets provided,) a pumpkin patch perfect for cozy fall photos and a shop on site where you can purchase fruit, syrup and gifts. Apple Land is for

51

anyone who loves cozy falls days and getting their hands a bit dirty for the sake of a great photo-op!

46. MAKE THE DETOUR TO HIT UP HEEMAN'S BERRY FARM

Heeman's is located a quick 15-20 minute drive from London in my hometown of Thorndale, but it is known to local Londoners and THE place to go for garden essentials and of course what they are most famous for... STRAWBERRIES! Starting in June and available until early fall, you must not make a trip to London without picking up a quart of these berries. If you're feeling a fun family activity, you can also opt for their U-Pick option. Plan to spend a few hours at this greenhouse... there is so much to see and do. In fact, you can fit two NFL football stadiums into the space at Heeman's greenhouse! Also make sure to try one their coffees or teas at the small café just inside the berry shop. They've got great customer service and are well-known for their berry sundaes (of which I have had a few (hundred) in my life!)

47. MAYBE LONDON, ENGLAND IS THE "OTHER" LONDON?

London England is known for the Thames River running through it, but it is worth noting that London, Ontario has a Thames of its own! Stretching from one end of the city to the other (and beyond) the Thames River is famous in our city. It contains 90 different species of fish and many birds which you can easily watch, especially at dawn or dusk. You can catch a glimpse of the river from many of the hiking trails including just about anywhere in Springbank Park, but you can also get a sensational view of it right from the downtown core. Many people stop at the Forks of The Thames for a photo-op, and certain times of year you can even watch the sun set over the river which is a real treat for locals and visitors alike.

London is also home to The Blackfriar's Bridge which is the oldest bridge of its kind in North America. It is the longest "bowstring arch through truss" bridge that can still be used to day and the area is which is it located is a great spot for picnics, long leisurely walks or bike rides.

48. FOUR SEASONS — THREE OF THEM ARE COLD!

Ontario sees all four seasons for about 4 months each, so it is worthwhile to check the weather before you travel. In peak summer months (July & August), we see temperatures in the 30s (Celsius) but in January-March, we might see several inches of snow and temperatures around -20 (Celsius.) During spring and fall, the temperature will fluctuate a lot, and it is not uncommon to have a heat wave AND a snow storm within the same week. Dress accordingly and make sure you always travel with warm clothes, year round!

49. LONDON PSYCHIATRIC HOSPITAL

What was once a working farm and psychiatric hospital is now an area which you can tour, take photos and take a history lesson. This area was active as the site for several psychiatric facilities in the city center in the early 1900's but the hospital has since been moved. The building remain and offer a spooky backdrop with abandoned buildings. The area itself is still open to the public and although I've never been brave enough to go, many locals do take tours (and night tours!) of the grounds for storytelling and even ghost hunting. If this is your thing, then this site was made for you. There is no cost and it is accessible by foot or vehicle.

50. WE ARE CALLED 'THE FOREST CITY' FOR A REASON!

London is known for being a "green" city and most citizens do not tolerate littering so please be mindful! We have an extensive and easy-to-use recycling program at most businesses and hotels, so recycling is always welcome, no matter where you are in the city.

London is surrounded by fields, green space and trees... in fact, when I asked my network of people what they liked best about living in London, more than half of them mentioned all the lush greenery around our city. Our government invests in planting trees and maintaining our green spaces, so if you're coming to hike or explore our parks and trails, make sure you leave them as pretty as they were when you got here! And if you're feeling extra green, London hosts plenty of 'clean up' days where folks volunteer to help pick up litter around our parks... this is a great opportunity to give back and feel like a REAL local.

TOP REASONS TO BOOK THIS TRIP

1.) London is surrounded by beautiful beaches (less than one hour away!), green spaces, parks and farm land. If you're seeking nature or outdoor activities, but also want to stay in a safe city, then London, Ontario is the place for you!

2.) Enjoy just about any kind of food or cultural experience, especially in the summer with our rotating schedule of summer festivals. Or try one of the many amazing ethnic food restaurants interspersed throughout the city.

3.) London is a safe, friendly, accessible and multicultural city that you can travel to with your family, pets or on your own. There are plenty of historical sites, heritage buildings, art and things to do around town no matter what time of year you come.

DID YOU KNOW?

-London has over 55 live music venues including The London Music Hall, Aeolian Hall and Centennial Hall

- There are over 140 languages spoken in London including Portuguese, Mandarin and Swiss

- London is ranked the 6th happiest city in Canada according to JetPac City Guides

- London is home of Plunket Estates, where Dr. Earl Plunket was said to have invented the birth control pill

- As of 2022, there were 78 Tim Horton's restaurants in London, Ontario

- It is believed that Hawaiian Pizza (Pineapple, ham and cheese) was invented in London's neighboring city, Chatham, Ontario, and the first pizzeria to sell this now famous pizza was located on Wellington Street in London

OTHER RESOURCES:

https://www.ledc.com/ London Economic Development Corp – helpful information for newcomers

https://london.ca/ Official website

https://www.londontourism.ca/ Tourism London for helpful tips

https://nationalpost.com/news/canada/the-time-johnny-cash-chose-an-ontario-hockey-arena-to-propose-to-june-carter The story of Johnny Cash in London

TRIVIA

1)   What 2004 romantic movie has not one but two famous actors born in London, Ontario?

2)   What is the average age of London resident?

3)   Who was London's first mayor?

4)   Who is the largest employer in London?

5)   Established in 1852, what is London's oldest bar?

6)   Who was the first performer to play at Budweiser Gardens when they opened in 2002 (formerly the John Labatt Center)?

7)   What is the oldest movie theater in London?

8)   Which London business was Canada's last indecently owned department store?

9)   What famous 50's themed diner is London's oldest restaurant?

10)   In 2018, which hospital used a robot for a landmark heart surgery top perform an aortic valve replacement?

ANSWERS

1) The Notebook (Ryan Gosling and Rachel McAdams)

2) 40.9

3) Murray Anderson

4) London Health Sciences Centre. It employs 10,555 people.

5) The Richmond Tavern

6) Our Lady Peace

7) The Palace Theater – opened in 1929!

8) Kingsmills was founded in 1865 and was open for 148 years before it finally sold in 2014.

9) Delmar – opened in 1953!

10) London's University Hospital

PACKING AND PLANNING TIPS

A Week before Leaving

- Arrange for someone to take care of pets and water plants.

- Email and Print important Documents.

- Get Visa and vaccines if needed.

- Check for travel warnings.

- Stop mail and newspaper.

- Notify Credit Card companies where you are going.

- Passports and photo identification is up to date.

- Pay bills.

- Copy important items and download travel Apps.

- Start collecting small bills for tips.

- Have post office hold mail while you are away.

- Check weather for the week.

- Car inspected, oil is changed, and tires have the correct pressure.

- Check airline luggage restrictions.

- Download Apps needed for your trip.

Right Before Leaving

- Contact bank and credit cards to tell them your location.

- Clean out refrigerator.

- Empty garbage cans.

- Lock windows.

- Make sure you have the proper identification with you.

- Bring cash for tips.

- Remember travel documents.

- Lock door behind you.

- Remember wallet.

- Unplug items in house and pack chargers.

- Change your thermostat settings.

- Charge electronics, and prepare camera memory cards.

READ OTHER GREATER THAN A TOURIST BOOKS

Greater Than a Tourist- California: 50 Travel Tips from Locals

Greater Than a Tourist- Salem Massachusetts USA 50 Travel Tips from a Local by Danielle Lasher

Greater Than a Tourist United States: 50 Travel Tips from Locals

Greater Than a Tourist- St. Croix US Birgin Islands USA: 50 Travel Tips from a Local by Tracy Birdsall

Greater Than a Tourist- Montana: 50 Travel Tips from a Local by Laurie White

Children's Book: Charlie the Cavalier Travels the World by Lisa Rusczyk Ed. D.

> TOURIST

Follow us on Instagram for beautiful travel images:
http://Instagram.com/GreaterThanATourist

Follow *Greater Than a Tourist* on Amazon.

CZYKPublishing.com

> TOURIST

At *Greater Than a Tourist*, we love to share travel tips with you. How did we do? What guidance do you have for how we can give you better advice for your next trip? Please send your feedback to CZYKPublishing@gmail.com as we continue to improve the series. We appreciate your constructive feedback. Thank you.

METRIC CONVERSIONS

TEMPERATURE

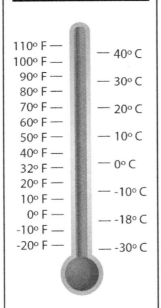

110° F	
100° F	— 40° C
90° F	— 30° C
80° F	
70° F	— 20° C
60° F	
50° F	— 10° C
40° F	
32° F	— 0° C
20° F	
10° F	— -10° C
0° F	
-10° F	— -18° C
-20° F	— -30° C

To convert F to C:

Subtract 32, and then multiply by 5/9 or .5555.

To Convert C to F:

Multiply by 1.8 and then add 32.

32F = 0C

LIQUID VOLUME

To Convert:..................Multiply by
U.S. Gallons to Liters................ 3.8
U.S. Liters to Gallons 26
Imperial Gallons to U.S. Gallons 1.2
Imperial Gallons to Liters....... 4.55
Liters to Imperial Gallons 22
1 Liter = .26 U.S. Gallon
1 U.S. Gallon = 3.8 Liters

DISTANCE

To convert ....Multiply by
Inches to Centimeters 2.54
Centimeters to Inches 39
Feet to Meters...................... .3
Meters to Feet 3.28
Yards to Meters 91
Meters to Yards 1.09
Miles to Kilometers 1.61
Kilometers to Miles............ .62
1 Mile = 1.6 km
1 km = .62 Miles

WEIGHT

1 Ounce = .28 Grams
1 Pound = .4555 Kilograms
1 Gram = .04 Ounce
1 Kilogram = 2.2 Pounds

TRAVEL QUESTIONS

- Do you bring presents home to family or friends after a vacation?

- Do you get motion sick?

- Do you have a favorite billboard?

- Do you know what to do if there is a flat tire?

- Do you like a sun roof open?

- Do you like to eat in the car?

- Do you like to wear sun glasses in the car?

- Do you like toppings on your ice cream?

- Do you use public bathrooms?

- Did you bring a cell phone and does it have power?

- Do you have a form of identification with you?

- Have you ever been pulled over by a cop?

- Have you ever given money to a stranger on a road trip?

- Have you ever taken a road trip with animals?

- Have you ever gone on a vacation alone?

- Have you ever run out of gas?

- If you could move to any place in the world, where would it be?

- If you could travel anywhere in the world, where would you travel?

- If you could travel in any vehicle, which one would it be?

- If you had three things to wish for from a magic genie, what would they be?

- If you have a driver's license, how many times did it take you to pass the test?

- What are you the most afraid of on vacation?

- What do you want to get away from the most when you are on vacation?

- What foods smell bad to you?

- What item do you bring on ever trip with you away from home?

- What makes you sleepy?

- What song would you love to hear on the radio when you're cruising on the highway?

- What travel job would you want the least?

- What will you miss most while you are away from home?

- What is something you always wanted to try?

- What is the best road side attraction that you ever saw?

- What is the farthest distance you ever biked?

- What is the farthest distance you ever walked?

- What is the weirdest thing you needed to buy while on vacation?

- What is your favorite candy?

- What is your favorite color car?

- What is your favorite family vacation?

- What is your favorite food?

- What is your favorite gas station drink or food?

- What is your favorite license plate design?

- What is your favorite restaurant?

- What is your favorite smell?

- What is your favorite song?

- What is your favorite sound that nature makes?

- What is your favorite thing to bring home from a vacation?

- What is your favorite vacation with friends?

- What is your favorite way to relax?

- Where is the farthest place you ever traveled in a car?

- Where is the farthest place you ever went North, South, East and West?

- Where is your favorite place in the world?

- Who is your favorite singer?

- Who taught you how to drive?

- Who will you miss the most while you are away?

- Who if the first person you will contact when you get to your destination?

- Who brought you on your first vacation?

- Who likes to travel the most in your life?

- Would you rather be hot or cold?

- Would you rather drive above, below, or at the speed limited?

- Would you rather drive on a highway or a back road?

- Would you rather go on a train or a boat?

- Would you rather go to the beach or the woods?

TRAVEL BUCKET LIST

1.

2.

3.

4.

5.

6.

7.

8.

9.

10.

NOTES

Printed in Great Britain
by Amazon